OECD Development Policy Tools

Using Extractive Revenues for Sustainable Development

POLICY GUIDANCE FOR RESOURCE-RICH COUNTRIES

This work is published under the responsibility of the Secretary-General of the OECD. The opinions expressed and arguments employed herein do not necessarily reflect the official views of the member countries of the OECD or its Development Centre.

This document, as well as any data and map included herein, are without prejudice to the status of or sovereignty over any territory, to the delimitation of international frontiers and boundaries and to the name of any territory, city or area.

Please cite this publication as:
OECD (2019), *Using Extractive Revenues for Sustainable Development : Policy Guidance for Resource-rich Countries*, OECD Development Policy Tools, OECD Publishing, Paris, *https://doi.org/10.1787/a9332691-en*.

ISBN 978-92-64-37109-5 (print)
ISBN 978-92-64-76944-1 (pdf)

OECD Development Policy Tools
ISSN 2518-6248 (print)
ISSN 2518-3702 (online)

Photo credits: Cover design by the OECD Development Centre based on images © m.wolf/shutterstock.com.

Corrigenda to publications may be found on line at: *www.oecd.org/about/publishing/corrigenda.htm*.
© OECD 2019

The use of this work, whether digital or print, is governed by the Terms and Conditions to be found at *http://www.oecd.org/termsandconditions*.

Foreword

This report was prepared by the OECD Development Centre within the framework of the Policy Dialogue on Natural Resource-based Development. It was welcomed by participants in the Eleventh Plenary of the Policy Dialogue on Natural Resource-based Development held on 12-13 December 2018 at the OECD in Paris.

This report rationalises the analysis developed for the Policy Dialogue's Work Stream 2 on Revenue Management and Spending between 2015-2018, also building on the lessons learned from the knowledge-sharing and peer-learning exercise in relation to the management and mobilisation of natural resource revenues to support the 2030 Agenda for Sustainable Development.

The first part of the report discusses key principles of the management of natural resource revenues for a sustainable budget. The second part discusses mechanisms for the mobilisation of natural resource revenues for sustainable development. The report concludes with recommended policy responses to key identified revenue management and spending challenges.

Table of Contents

Executive summary 6

Introduction 8

1. How to manage natural resource revenues to ensure fiscal sustainability 10

Key attributes of non-renewable natural resource revenues 10
The importance of a clear commitment to a coherent, consistent and disciplined fiscal policy
and macroeconomic management framework 10
Stabilisation funds as an integral part of the fiscal policy and macroeconomic management
framework 10

2. How to spend natural resource revenues for sustainable development 18

Addressing the trade-off between saving and spending natural resource revenues 18
Prioritising development without earmarking natural resource revenues 22
Assessing direct distribution mechanisms 26
Strategic investment funds as emerging tools for extra-budgetary investment 30

3. Key policy recommendations 36

Policy Challenge 1: How to reconcile long-term development and intergenerational equity
objectives with the need to manage the volatility and uncertainty of exhaustible resource
revenues 36
Policy Challenge 2: How to transform finite natural resource revenues into long-standing and
productive development gains, in order to put resource-rich developing countries on a
sustainable development trajectory that outlives resource extraction. 37
Notes 38
References 41

Figures

Figure 2.1. Addressing the trade-off between saving and spending 20

Boxes

Box 1.1. Learning from investment governance failures 15
Box 1.2. Employing disclosure mechanisms for transparency and accountability 16
Box 2.1. Moving from prudent fiscal management to a countercyclical fiscal policy in Kazakhstan 19
Box 2.2. Saving for future generations in Norway 20
Box 2.3. The pitfalls of earmarking natural resource revenues 24
Box 2.4. Mongolia's experience with resources-to-cash 29
Box 2.5. Collaboration and co-investment in Russia 33

Executive summary

Non-renewable natural resource revenues can make an important contribution to harnessing inclusive growth and sustainable development, provided that resource revenues are appropriately managed to smooth revenue flows throughout the price cycle and effectively spent domestically to transform finite natural resource revenues into long-standing and productive development gains. Since 2013, the OECD Development Centre's Policy Dialogue on Natural Resource-based Development has fostered peer-learning and experience sharing on trade-offs, advantages and disadvantages of natural resource revenue management and spending mechanisms to use natural resource revenues to support the implementation of the 2030 Sustainable Development Agenda, drawing lessons from country experiences. The first challenge for policy makers is to reconcile long-term development and intergenerational equity objectives with the need to manage the volatility and uncertainty of exhaustible resource revenues. The establishment of a clear and consistent fiscal policy framework coupled with a commitment to sound macroeconomic management of natural resource revenues with properly sized stabilisation funds can help to insulate the economy from price, production or other external shocks and ensure medium- and long-term fiscal sustainability that supports long-term development objectives. In order to achieve the desired objectives, stabilisation funds need to be integrated into the budget through clear rules regarding the deposit of natural resource revenues, and the withdrawal of money for use in government spending and investment. Stabilisation funds provide a financial buffer when commodity markets collapse and revenues from natural resources decline. The investment management and governance of stabilisation funds need to support their budget stabilisation objectives. This means designing stabilisation funds to be fit for purpose with adequate human resourcing in relation to the level of risk taken to achieve their policy objectives, investment decision making that is free from political influence, and clear mechanisms providing transparency and accountability. As a source of precautionary savings, stabilisation funds should be invested in safe foreign assets to ensure sufficient liquidity to counter price volatility. Stabilisation funds are not effective vehicles for helping satisfy domestic capital needs, particularly in capital-starved developing economies where domestic assets are likely to be highly correlated with commodity prices given the structure of resource-dependent economies. Beyond the appropriate level of precautionary savings necessary to provide a financial buffer to ensure fiscal sustainability over time, resource-rich countries need to manage the trade-off between investing in the domestic economy or abroad, and saving for future generations. The country-specific development needs and circumstances should be reflected in how this trade-off is managed. The fiscal rules can be designed to favour current and medium-term expenditure of natural resource revenues or accumulate wealth for future generations in a savings fund in a manner that is consistent with national priorities and absorptive capacity constraints. When prioritising domestic investment, spending mechanisms that encourage procyclicality in public expenditures should be avoided as this exacerbates the effects of commodity price volatility on the economy. Earmarking can encourage procyclicality and constrain budgetary flexibility, leading to inefficiency and over or underinvestment in certain public services. Without concomitant stabilisation mechanisms, direct distribution through cash transfers is also highly procyclical and may divert revenues from priority investments at scale such as in infrastructure, health, and education. At the same time, targeted cash-transfer schemes that operate through the government budget may be useful to smooth the transition for gradually phasing out fossil fuel subsidies, which tend to be poorly targeted and inefficient, yet popularly supported and thus often difficult to reform. Policy makers need to ensure the quality and efficiency of public investment spending to translate natural resource wealth into productive capital accumulation, leading to broader development gains. Strategic investment funds can help natural resource-rich countries manage long-term financing challenges and shrinking fiscal space, while balancing policy and commercial objectives. This can be done by leveraging private capital to kick-start productive growth and development, through reinforcing, renewing and reorganising state assets, crowding-in investments, catalysing new economic opportunities and supporting local financial-market development. With their double bottom-line objective, whereby all investment decisions must fulfil market-based risk and return criteria, and produce positive development outcomes, strategic investment funds offer a possible tool for resource-rich countries to catalyse economic development, alongside conventional spending via the budget. Such funds are most effective as part of a clear government investment policy that establishes the priorities, criteria and targets for investment, coupled with some level of co-ordination across government levels and different agencies to avoid duplication of public investment. Effectiveness is also supported by the capacity to build a professional and capable investment team to further scrutinise the financial and economic feasibility and sustainability of public investment projects, coupled with adherence to accepted standards of disclosure and transparency. However, experience with such funds in developing countries is still limited.

Introduction

The aim of this report is to distil lessons from the experience-sharing and peer-learning process of the OECD Policy Dialogue on Natural Resource-based Development on natural resource revenue management and spending. Two principal concerns underlie the challenge of transforming natural finite assets into human, social and physical capital: managing the counter-cyclical nature of resource revenue flows to ensure that there is a consistent level of resources available for spending; and ensuring productive gains from the funds that are spent, in line with the 2030 Sustainable Development Agenda.

The first part of this report identifies the main lessons from peer-learning exercises on how to manage natural resource revenues through the establishment and good governance of stabilisation funds. These mechanisms support the objectives of fiscal sustainability and macroeconomic stability as a basis for efficient public spending and government decision making over time. The second part of the report focuses on how natural resource revenues can be spent to support sustainable development objectives through an appropriate fiscal policy framework that considers the level of savings necessary to ensure stability of spending over the commodity price cycle, the time horizon of natural resource production and the absorptive capacity of the economy.

The second part is divided into four sections. The first section addresses the trade-offs of spending more now versus savings. This decision is country-specific and it should reflect countries' development needs. In general, poorer countries should emphasise sustainable development spending rather than saving but conforming with the absorptive capacity of the economy and the deepening of the financial market, whereas higher income countries should prioritise savings. In both cases, the time horizon of natural resource production matters, where a short time horizon skews the decision towards savings and a long time horizon skews the decision towards spending.

The second section shows that earmarking natural resource revenues for specific spending items is not necessary to ensure spending is focused on sustainable development outcomes, as the experiences of Botswana and Indonesia show. The evidence on the effectiveness of earmarking is, in contrast, mixed and in some cases highly negative.

The third section considers the pros and cons of using direct distribution schemes that allocate resource revenues to the population. While there are potential benefits in terms of mobilising citizen support for managing natural resource revenues effectively, there is insufficient evidence to recommend natural resource producing countries experiment with them. A better option, as the case of Timor-Leste suggests, are targeted cash transfer schemes that operate via the budget. This option assumes, however, that the natural resource revenues entering the budget are managed sustainably.

The fourth section reviews the emerging trend of some countries, including natural resource-rich countries, of establishing strategic investment funds to facilitate diversification of the domestic economy. Strategic investment funds adopt the practices and methods of similar investment funds operating in the private sector, but invest with the aim of generating both a financial return and a developmental return.

1. How to manage natural resource revenues to ensure fiscal sustainability

Key attributes of non-renewable natural resource revenues

There are three key attributes of non-renewable natural resource revenues. First, they are intrinsically temporary in that they result from the depletion of a finite stock of resources, with a greater or lesser production horizon depending on accessibility, quality of ores and technological developments (Fasano-Filho, 2000; Solow, 1986). Second, given that commodity prices can be highly volatile and prone to booms and busts, they are an unreliable source of income. Natural resource revenue windfalls may lead to a more-than-proportional increase in discretionary spending that magnifies the pro-cyclicality of the economy, leading to a deterioration of government accounts and subsequently to increased debt accumulation and higher borrowing costs (Tornell and Lane, 1999). Third, natural resource revenues, particularly in the context of large windfalls and strong global demand, can also place strong upward pressure on the national currency and domestic prices (Gylfason, 2001). Consequently, the inflationary pressures from natural resource production can constrain the competitiveness in global and regional markets of other sectors of the economy, such as manufacturing and agriculture. This distorts the economy and limits potential diversification, which may provide greater opportunities and a broader base for socio-economic development. This effect is generally referred to as "Dutch disease" (Corden, 1984).

The importance of a clear commitment to a coherent, consistent and disciplined fiscal policy and macroeconomic management framework

Given these attributes of natural resource revenues, two principal concerns underlie the challenge of effectively transforming natural finite assets into human, social and physical capital: 1) managing the counter-cyclical nature of resource revenue flows to ensure that there is a consistent level of resources available for spending; and 2) ensuring productive gains from the funds that are spent, in line with the 2030 Sustainable Development Agenda.

While experience varies across producing countries, a sensible approach for resource-dependent countries is to establish earlier rather than later a clear resource revenue management framework and fiscal policy that stabilises the budget and appreciates the country-specific trade-offs of more spending or more saving over time, and how doing so can support the growth of a more sustainable diversified economy.

Stabilisation funds as an integral part of the fiscal policy and macroeconomic management framework

Stabilisation funds are a possible tool to achieve budget stabilisation. According to the IMF, countries that would benefit from the establishment of stabilisation funds are those that are resource dependent as they derive at least 20% of their revenue from natural resources and need to counter the cyclical component linked to the commodity cycle (see e.g. Das et al., 2010). Indeed, the main challenge for policy makers in resource-dependent countries is dealing with the volatility of prices.

While stabilisation funds act to dampen volatility by smoothing out the revenues received by the government, they should not be expected to operate and achieve their policy objectives in isolation. Stabilisation funds are only effective and sustainable over time as part of a coherent and disciplined fiscal policy framework. Stabilisation funds are a tool in a broader macroeconomic management framework that needs to be coherent, consistent and disciplined. This means that stabilisation funds *should be integrated* with the budget through deposit and withdrawal rules and procedures on how much and when withdrawals can be made to the government budget, which are rigorously articulated and defined in the legislative mandate. Establishment of the fiscal policy framework and connected stabilisation fund should occur before production commences, or as soon as possible thereafter.

Chile demonstrates policy coherence, consistency and commitment with regard to managing the volatility of commodity prices (see e.g. Frankel, 2010). Authorised by the 2006 Fiscal Responsibility Law, Chile established in 2007 the *Fondo de Estabilización Económica y Social* (FEES), a stabilisation fund with the purpose of financing budget deficits that result from the economic cycle or international shocks that may affect the price of copper – the country's main export (Frankel, 2010). Chile's FEES achieves its policy objective through clearly defined deposit and withdrawal rules and complete integration with the budget.

Since its inception, FEES has mainly been used for financing the fiscal deficit in 2009 and as a countercyclical stimulus for addressing the external economic shocks that followed the 2008 global financial crisis. This reinforced public support for the fund and its mission to support the Chilean economy across society, countering previous pressure from different political actors to use the fund's resources. Continued support was also shown in the new coalition government that assumed power in 2010 leaving the fiscal policy framework and fund's operation unchanged. The FEES has thus performed well in its function of stabilising government spending across the economic cycle, while expenditure rules have limited the volatility of natural resource revenues from entering the budget.

Chile's FEES, for example, receives any effective fiscal surplus beyond 0.5% of GDP from the previous year. The FEES may also receive resources from the issuance of debt or other resources that may be contributed by law. Moreover, annual fiscal expenditure is contingent on permanent fiscal revenues and the balanced budget rule. The estimation of permanent fiscal revenue is based on the forecast of the price of copper (the average for the next ten years) and the growth trend of the Chilean economy. Two expert committees that are independent of government carry out the forecasts of the price of copper and of the inputs to estimate the growth trend of the economy. This limits any potential manipulation. Legislation authorises the Chilean Minister of Finance to define the timing and the amount of withdrawals, and then publicly disclose this information. Withdrawals are publicly disclosed in a clear manner and must be authorised by decree by the Minister of Finance. They are implemented by the Central Bank and the General Treasury and are subject to review by the Comptroller General's Office.

Consistency over time, commitment and policy alignment support the effectiveness of the stabilisation fund at fulfilling its policy objective, namely budget stabilisation. This means that other policies and financial commitments should not overlap with the policy purpose of the stabilisation fund. For example, there is no economic sense in putting aside natural resource revenues in a stabilisation fund and then increasing government debt if the risk-adjusted returns of the stabilisation fund are lower than the interest costs of the government debt. Finally, as one of the main aims of stabilisation funds is to reduce the effects of commodity price volatility and address the exhaustibility of natural resource revenues, this calls for consistency and commitment across multiple years in the establishment and maintenance of the fiscal rules and procedures that underwrite the policy objectives.

Withdrawal rules may not, however, be able to account for all contingencies where withdrawals are legitimate. Large and unexpected negative shocks can arise from economic sources and natural disasters. Making extraordinary withdrawals to mitigate and stabilise the effects of unforeseen events is a justifiable use of a stabilisation fund. Although extraordinary and unforeseen events by their nature cannot be planned for, the process and procedural rules by which extraordinary spending is decided can be (Ang, 2010). As such, this provides an additional commitment mechanism by forcing the justification of discretionary withdrawals and requiring that they be tied to extraordinary events.

The size of the stabilisation fund

The amount of resources to be put in stabilisation funds depends on the exhaustibility of resources and the price formula which varies across countries. There is no absolute size for a stabilisation fund. Rather, the size will reflect the policy choices that determine how much revenues should be saved and for how long (see also the first section of part two of this report on the trade-off between saving and spending natural resource revenues).

The investment policy should be aligned with the budget stabilisation policy objective

Stabilisation funds are sponsored by governments with the purpose of stabilising the regular inflow of natural resource revenues into the government budget. The policy objective of budget stabilisation should dictate the investment policy, as evidence shows that alignment of the investment policy with the policy objective supports the effectiveness of the investment function. The investment policy that the government sets acts to guide the asset allocation of the fund, setting performance benchmarks, the level of risk that can be taken, and the assets in which the fund can be invested. The investment policy can be defined by strict rules, or it can be based on principles such as the prudent person rule. The investment policy could also be a combination of strict rules and principles.

Stabilisation funds by design should have an investment policy that limits investment to low-risk and highly liquid fixed-income securities and cash. In fact, the key objective of the stabilisation fund is not to maximise returns, but rather hedge fiscal revenues against fluctuation of commodity prices. For stabilisation funds, investing in safe foreign assets is necessary to ensure sufficient liquidity to counter price volatility. Stabilisation funds are not effective vehicles for helping satisfy domestic capital needs, particularly in capital-starved developing economies where domestic assets are likely to be highly correlated with commodity prices given the structure of resource-dependent economies. In such contexts, the formula for allocating natural resource revenues (the deposit and withdrawal rules) can be designed in such a way to favour current spending via the budget over the accumulation of savings beyond what is necessary to support stabilisation and short to medium-term precautionary savings.

Resource-dependent developed and developing economies alike may be exposed to criticism for pursuing a conservative investment policy when returns on investment are low (e.g. depreciations of foreign currencies) or in capital-starved contexts. In this respect, transparency is an important tool, not just to report on performance, but more importantly to build trust among citizens and educate the public and stakeholders on what and why conservative investment policies have been put in place in the first instance (see Box 1.2).

Investment management of stabilisation funds

The effectiveness of a natural resource fund as an institutional investor is supported by a portfolio asset allocation that reflects the weight and risk profile of the fund's policy objective(s). For example, some governments have tasked natural resource funds with achieving multiple policy objectives. This could pose problems, as different policy objectives can have different organisational resourcing needs and a different investment focus and time horizon. As such, a fund that is designed to deal efficiently with one objective may not be able to adequately and efficiently handle problems and challenges (or opportunities) that arise from another set of objectives, such as having sufficient short-term liquidity to fulfil a stabilisation mandate while also maximising the risk-adjusted return on intergenerational savings. Hence, some governments avoid this dilemma by limiting the investment scope and organisational structure of a fund to a single policy objective. For example, Chile created two funds, namely the Pension Reserve Fund and the Economic and Social Stabilization Fund. Before the crisis the stabilisation fund had accumulated assets for USD 20 billion. Almost half of the fund was used to counter the consequences of the financial crisis.

This dilemma could be accounted for if, however, the investment mandate and in turn the asset allocation of the portfolio clearly reflects the weight and risk profile of each policy objective. For instance, a long-term savings fund could still hold a percentage of highly liquid low-risk assets in its portfolio, which allows the fund to double as a precautionary savings fund. Or, the fund could simply have two distinct portfolios. The National Fund of the Republic of Kazakhstan (NFRK) is an example of a natural resource fund that covers two policy objectives (stabilisation and savings) via two distinct portfolios of different time horizons, instead of two distinct funds. The stabilisation portfolio, accounting for 32% of the total market value of the NFRK assets, has a short time horizon and is invested in highly liquid assets (e.g. US Treasury securities). The savings portfolio has a long time horizon and is invested in developed capital markets with 80% in fixed income and 20% in equities. Investments in Kazakhstan are prohibited.

Although stabilisation funds are by design cautious and risk-intolerant institutional investors, the alignment of the investment mandate with the policy objectives is no less critical to effective performance than a more sophisticated institutional investor. Chile demonstrates adherence to this principle. The main goal of the investment policy of Chile's FEES is to maximise the fund's accumulated value in order to partially cover cyclical reductions in fiscal revenue, while maintaining a low level of risk. The investment policy explicitly states that the investment should be passive, tracking widely used market benchmarks, and that the portfolio managers should not deviate from those. The asset allocation set in the investment policy is 55% sovereign bonds, 34% money market instruments (15% in bank deposits and 19% in sovereign securities), 7.5% in equities and 3.5% in inflation-indexed sovereign bonds. No securities should be emitted by a Chilean entity. The currency composition is specified as 40% in dollars, 25% in euros, 20% in yen and 7.5% in Swiss francs for the fixed-income portfolio, expressed as a percentage of the total portfolio. Each asset class is benchmarked to a widely used market benchmark.

Since the creation of the FEES in 2007, only one review of the investment policy has been carried out (in 2013) with a view to improving its consistency with the goals of the fund. Review of the investment policy is expected to take place every three or four years. The investment policy proved to be successful in the wake of the global financial crisis, as the fund was invested in securities denominated in reserve currencies that benefited from flight-to-quality effects and that were highly liquid, which facilitated the withdrawal when the government needed the resources. Put simply, the clear alignment of the investment policy with the policy objectives set for the FEES meant that the fund could fulfil its objective function of providing precautionary savings in a time of crisis.

With savings funds, in contrast, the longer time horizon inherent to the policy objective in principle affords a lower liquidity preference and a greater risk tolerance. For example, a savings fund that aims to maximise the value of accumulated natural resource wealth for future generations would have a time horizon that, in theory, spans decades or even into perpetuity. In that case, the fund would be in a position to invest for the long and very long term (i.e. decades). This means that the fund would not be under pressure to sell assets during periods of poor market performance and it would be able to invest without concern for short-term liquidity. In brief, the fund could invest in asset classes that are more volatile and riskier in the short term (e.g. equities) but that yield a greater long-term return (see, Dimson, Marsh, and Staunton, 2002; Fama and French, 2002; Goetzmann and Ibbotson, 2006). This rationale underpins the investment strategy Norway's Government Pension Fund–Global, which has a portfolio that is heavily invested in global equities markets (Chambers, Dimson, and Ilmanen, 2012). The understanding is that although equities markets are more volatile in the short term, they are mean reverting and higher yielding over time than lower-risk fixed-income securities. *Evidence shows that long-term value creation is contingent on the management of risk and uncertainty*. Poorly governed investment institutions rarely take risk planning seriously and they insufficiently resource (with time and expertise) the investment decision-making process in relation to the level of risks that the fund is taking (Clark and Urwin, 2008). Good investment governance practices, in contrast, generate positive financial returns (see e.g. Ambachtsheer, Capelle, and Scheibelhut, 1998; Ammann and Zingg, 2010; Iglesias and Palacios, 2000; Mitchell and Hsin, 1997). The level of acceptable risk taken should be contingent on the organisational and human resources capabilities.[1]

Governance of natural resource funds

As pools of financial assets, natural resource stabilisation and savings funds are institutional investors. As such, there are important considerations as to how they are governed as financial institutions. Weak investment governance can lead to significant financial losses, while undermining the stabilisation function of the fund (see Box 1.1).

> **Box 1.1. Learning from investment governance failures**
>
> An exemplary case of poor investment governance is the Libyan Investment Authority (LIA), as documented by Khalaf et al. (2011) and Saigol and O'Murchu (2011). Established in 2006 with USD 65 billion, the LIA set out to be a world-class institutional investor investing across asset classes and international markets. What resulted was a series of opaque and high-risk investments in hedge funds and complex derivative transactions. Although the LIA had committed financial professionals, evidence suggests that a close-knit group with close ties to Seif Gaddafi (Muammar Gaddafi's son) decided most deals. Many deals were loss making. Some investments were run through or advised by firms of Libyan elites that were well connected to the Gaddafi family, who were also paid large management fees, indicating possible corruption and misappropriation.

Governance as it relates to institutional investment funds refers to the structure, process and practices that establish the relationship between the owner/sponsor of the fund, the board of directors, the management, and any third-party asset manager, and the criteria that guide investment decision making. In short, the governance architecture dictates how external and internal authority is utilised and how financial capital is distributed and mobilised in pursuit of institutional objectives (i.e. the policy objectives set forth in its establishment and their associated investment criteria).

Evidence shows that investment decision making shielded from short-term political cycles drives better performance. It is crucial for the success of natural resource funds, as with any public institutional investor (e.g. a public pension fund) that they are free from unwarranted political interference and influence. Indeed, research has shown that political interference in investment decision making can result in financial damage (see e.g. Romano, 1993). This is distinct from the sponsoring authority's (e.g. the parliament, Ministry of Finance, etc.) role and responsibility in establishing the broader aims, objectives and restrictions as defined in the investment mandate.

Interference is mitigated by leaving investment decision making, such as specific decisions on asset allocation and manager selection, to an independent board that is charged with operationalising the investment mandate and any other guidelines that the sponsor has established. This also means that appointments to key decision-making bodies are decided on the basis of one's domain-specific expertise and experience, and not on the basis of one's personal connections (Clark, 2007). Investment decision making should be guided by independent and professional experts that are free of direct political influence, and with clear boundaries defining the separation, and the roles and responsibilities of the fund's sponsor, the board, and the fund's manager, with a view to ensuring that the funds are insulated from the short-term political cycle and political interference, especially when conservative and risk intolerant asset allocation shifts towards more diversified investment strategy in order to maximise long-term risk-adjusted returns.

Disclosure mechanisms that provide key information on key decisions (e.g. manager selection, board appointments, asset allocation) and financial performance, which are regularly and independently audited for consistency and reliability, are also important for driving better performance. Transparency and accountability, which are operationalised through regular reporting and auditing practices, are crucial for efficient budgetary and investment functions of the natural resource fund. Good practice entails extensive (and duplicative) internal and external oversight across all levels (see Box 1.2). This drives better decision making and better behaviour among those that have been tasked with managing a country's national wealth. Disclosure and regular auditing help prevent mismanagement and potential malfeasance.

For example, **Mexico** follows good practice in the governance of its new natural resource fund established in 2015, the *Fondo Mexicano del Petróleo para la Estabilización y el Desarrollo* (FMP). Mexico has placed significant emphasis on ensuring that the members of the technical committee, which is the board of the FMP, possess sufficient domain-specific expertise and experience.[2] Although the technical committee is composed of three government representatives, the Minister of Finance (president of the committee), the Minister of Energy and the Governor of the Central Bank, the technical committee also has four independent members that are appointed by the federal executive and ratified by two-thirds of the senate. To be eligible, the independent members must have a professional title (bachelor's degree) no less than ten years old at the day of the appointment in any of the following areas: law, management, economics, finance, accountancy, actuarial science, engineering or subjects related to the FMP. And, they must have served for at least ten years in activities that provide the necessary experience and are related to the functions of the committee, either in the professional, educational or research areas. Independent members are elected for staggered eight-year terms with the possibility of re-election. Moreover, independent members must not have been a public servant at any level of government, have held elective positions, or have been directors of any political party during the two years prior to appointment. They must not hold other positions in government and may not develop activities in the private sector, which involve a conflict of interest. They must not hold simultaneous positions or employment that prevent the exercise of their function as independent members. Moreover, they must not have been a shareholder, partner or owner, officer, director, legal representative or advisor of any assignee or contractor in the two years prior to their appointment or have pending litigation with any assignee or contractor at the day of the designation.

Box 1.2. Employing disclosure mechanisms for transparency and accountability

Externally, transparency and accountability are vital for sustaining on-going public confidence in the fund's policy objectives and the investment mandate, particularly in the context of democratic governance. Transparency is also important for ensuring international legitimacy, allowing natural resource funds unconstrained access to global financial markets and potentially investment partnerships necessary for achieving target financial returns and sufficient risk management opportunities. Without unconstrained access to investment and risk management opportunities, the fund may not be able to achieve its return targets and therefore the policy objectives it is supposed to support. Transparency is also critical to the internal operations of the fund and its relationship with the sponsor. The sponsor must be clear in the expectations it sets for the fund, otherwise those charged with executing the investment mandate may not be able to align the investment mandate with the policy objectives it is supposed to serve, thus reducing its effectiveness. Likewise, the fund and its managers must be transparent to the sponsor so that the sponsor is able to monitor effectively that the fund is meeting the objectives and expectations that the sponsor has set for the fund and that the fund continues to align with wider public financial management and fiscal policy. Transparency and accountability are crucial in preventing mismanagement and potential malfeasance. Consequently, a robust disclosure and audit framework is necessary for guiding functional efficiency, and policy and operational alignment and commitment over the long term (Gelpern, 2011).

Natural resource revenue management in Chile demonstrates good practice in terms of transparency and accountability, which underpins the functional efficiency and continued public legitimacy of the FEES. In order to ensure a proper and effective accountability framework, a range of reports are prepared by the different bodies and stakeholders involved in the FEES's management. The Ministry of Finance is required by law to provide the Finance Commissions of both houses of Congress and the Joint Budget Commission of Congress, monthly and quarterly reports about the fund. The Financial Committee supporting the Ministry of Finance also prepares a publicly available annual report about its activities and recommendations, which is presented to the Minister of Finance, the Finance Commissions of both houses of Congress and the Joint Budget Commission of Congress. The Central Bank provides the Ministry of Finance with daily, monthly, quarterly and annual reports about the portfolios under their management, and the services provided by the custodian. External managers must also provide the Ministry of Finance with daily and monthly reports about the portfolios under their management. As of 2011, the General Treasury, which is a dependent organisation of the Ministry of Finance, prepares the financial statements according to International Financial Reporting Standards (IFRS). The financial statements are independently audited in keeping with Chilean auditing standards. As of April 2014, the General Treasury is also responsible for monitoring compliance with the FEES's investment guidelines, validating external managers' fees, and other back office tasks. In addition, the Comptroller General's Office, an autonomous body, is responsible for auditing all public sector finances and, therefore, the FEES. In addition, and although not mandated by law, the Finance Ministry publishes an annual report about the FEES, which is publicly available.

2. How to spend natural resource revenues for sustainable development

Addressing the trade-off between saving and spending natural resource revenues

Once resource-dependent countries establish a minimum stabilisation function, they can explore how to find the right balance between saving and spending. In defining an appropriate country-specific fiscal policy framework for natural resource revenue management, there is a trade-off between spending more now versus saving for future generations. Not all countries may deem it beneficial to save natural resource revenues beyond what is necessary to ensure stability over the short to medium term (i.e. across the commodity price cycle). In other words, it may be in some countries' interest to spend now as much revenue as the stability mechanism allows rather than saving more revenues for future generations.

Studies have argued that capital-starved resource-rich developing economies should increase their utilisation of natural resource revenues in the domestic economy (see e.g. Baunsgaard et al. 2012, Collier et al. 2010, van der Ploeg and Venables, 2011). Poorer countries should spend more and save less to develop their economies. One method to address this challenge through stabilisation funds would be to design the formula for allocating natural resource revenues (the deposit and withdrawal rules) to favour current spending via the budget over the accumulation of savings beyond what is necessary to support stabilisation and short to medium-term precautionary savings. The need to address capital scarcity would also seem to suggest that natural resource funds should invest in domestic assets. But natural resource funds may not be the most effective vehicles for helping satisfy domestic capital needs, particularly in capital-starved developing economies.

Rules can be designed to prioritise savings at the expense of greater current spending, or vice versa, and should reflect the development level and needs of a country in relation to the time horizon of natural resource production. Kazakhstan provides an interesting example of how to move progressively from prudent fiscal management to a more balanced countercyclical fiscal policy (see Box 2.1). However, even if a country would like to spend more now, the economy may not be able to absorb quickly and productively the increased spending and investment. Hence, there may be sound reasons for a developing country to save more of current revenues until they can be utilised more productively and sustainably.

Box 2.1. Moving from prudent fiscal management to a countercyclical fiscal policy in Kazakhstan

In 2000, Kazakhstan established the National Fund of the Republic of Kazakhstan (NFRK) with a goal of reducing the government's dependence on resource revenues, to shield the economy from unfavourable external shocks, and to accumulate savings for future generations. In the first ten years of the fund, however, the NFRK was not on a sound footing in relation to the level of withdrawals.

In 2010, the "New Concept" for the NFRK was implemented to ensure its long-term viability (Kemme 2012). The New Concept fixed the withdrawals, known as guaranteed transfers, from the NFRK to the budget at USD 8 billion plus/minus 15% depending on the economic cycle. The level of the withdrawal was also made contingent on the balance of the NFRK remaining above 30% of GDP; and a target size of USD 180 billion was also set for the NFRK to be reached by 2020. The New Concept also allowed for targeted transfers for socially important large-scale projects in the absence of alternative financing at the request of the President, with the important caveat that these transfers go through the budget to ensure transparency. Finally, the New Concept introduced government debt financing maximums that are linked to the NFRK revenues. Specifically, the annual cost of servicing government debt must not exceed the annual conditional fixed investment income of the NFRK of 4.5%, and the annual cost of servicing and repayment of government debt should not exceed 15% of government revenues, including transfers from the NFRK.

In short, the overarching goals of the NFRK of stabilisation and savings did not change, but the New Concept placed greater pressure on the parliament to balance the government budget, with a target of limiting the non-oil deficit to 2.8% of GDP by 2020. The aim was to use oil revenues entering the budget to help finance and achieve the strategic development goals outlined by President Nursultan Nazarbayev in "Kazakhstan 2050" and the mid-term goals outlined in "Kazakhstan 2020". The strategic plan called for major political, social and economic reforms and investments with the aim of making Kazakhstan one of the top 30 global economies by 2050. Improving the country's infrastructure, driving growth of the private sector and increasing non-energy exports are among some of the goals.

Restrained expenditure growth since 2010 suggests that the New Concept has led to greater fiscal discipline, while preserving the continued growth of the assets of the NFRK. Yet, fiscal constraint could be explained by the lower economic growth and inflation during the period, and lower tax receipts. Even then, the progress made by Kazakhstan, which the evidence supports, demonstrates a broader commitment to a coherent, consistent, and disciplined fiscal policy and macroeconomic management framework to underwrite the effectiveness of the NFRK in achieving its stated policy objectives.

However, Kazakhstan's fiscal rules have been subject to criticism by international organisations for being too strict and preventing budgetary adjustments and counter-cyclicality, and creating potential room for political interference and discretionality in fiscal management. As a consequence, Kazakhstan is planning to introduce automatic stabilisers to automatically save more when commodity prices are high and transfer more in case of a downturn and a decrease of commodity prices.

One way of approaching this trade-off between saving and spending is to consider: 1) the capital stock and level of development of a country, 2) whether resource revenues are long lasting or temporary. Understanding the interplay between these two factors helps account for the differences between advanced and developing economies and their relative needs in terms of sustainable economic growth and development, and between countries where resource revenues are temporary and where resource revenues are longer lasting (see Baunsgaard et al. 2012). This results in four policy trajectories, which lead to greater or lesser savings (see Figure 2.1). As such, there is no absolute size for a stabilisation or a savings fund. Rather, the size is contingent on policy choices that determine how much revenue should be saved and for how long. The size of a fund is contingent on the prevailing price of the relevant natural resource over time. Countries where there is ample capital and where resource revenues are temporary may consider accumulating sufficient financial savings for future generations. A country in this situation is Norway, which has followed this path and has accumulated significant long-term savings (see Box 2.2).

Figure 2.1. Addressing the trade-off between saving and spending

	Temporary	Long term
High	Save for future generations (e.g. Norway)	Macroeconomic stability (e.g. Saudi Arabia, Kuwait)
Low	Domestic investment/ Saving for future (e.g. Timor-Leste)	Domestic investment & Macroeconomic stability (e.g. Nigeria)

Capital stock and level of development (y-axis) / *Time horizon of natural resources revenues* (x-axis)

Source: Adapted from Baunsgaard et al. 2012.

Box 2.2. Saving for future generations in Norway

In 1990 Norway established the Government Petroleum Fund, renamed the Government Pension Fund-Global (GPF-G) in 2006, to mitigate the macroeconomic effects of hydrocarbon revenues and to ensure intergenerational savings. Norway follows a financing fund approach. With financing funds, net inflows mirror the overall budget balance. All government revenues from oil and gas production, whether through taxation or ownership, less investment costs, are transferred to the fund from the budget. The fund through a reverse transfer finances the budget's non-oil deficit. In effect, the net flows of the fund are connected to the overall fiscal surplus or deficit.

> Norway utilises a fiscal guideline, set in 2001, that requires that the non-oil structural deficit of the central government not exceed 4% of the assets of the GPF, derived from the estimated long-run real rate of return with positive spill overs on the stability of the exchange rate. The guidelines allow for temporary deviations from this benchmark under special circumstances. While Norway is highly dependent on oil revenues, it has the world's biggest sovereign wealth fund with financial assets of USD 1 trillion representing 2.5 times Norway's GDP.
>
> The GPF-G owns approximately 2% of public equities globally. The fund was initially created for stabilisation purposes based on the basic principle of separating decisions on income generation from those about spending. Following steady increases in commodity prices, policy objectives gradually shifted from stabilisation to saving purposes. No investment can be made in the country. These rules have contributed so far to ensuring a predictable fiscal environment with the creation of stable conditions for the internationalisation of the oil and gas industry and they have insulated the domestic economy from inflationary pressure.

For countries where capital is scarce and where resource revenues are temporary, a balance should be struck between accumulating financial savings and spending resource revenue domestically to increase non-resource sector growth. Diversifying the economy has the added benefit of cushioning and stabilising the economy during periods of low performance in the extractives sector. However, the decision to save for future generations must also be set against the country's cost of borrowing. If the risk-adjusted returns of a savings fund are less than the country's borrowing costs, then there is limited economic rationale in accumulating long-term savings.

Ghana is an example of a country that is facing this policy dilemma. In 2007, a major offshore oil deposit, the Jubilee field, was discovered with an estimated 3 billion barrels. To manage this new revenue stream, Ghana created the Petroleum Holding Fund and the Ghana Petroleum Funds in 2011. All oil and gas revenues go directly to the Petroleum Holding Fund. Part of the revenue is then reinvested in the Ghana National Petroleum Corporation (GNPC). Another share is allocated to the Ghana Petroleum Funds which serve the dual objective of saving for future generations (Heritage Fund) and smoothing the effects of commodity price volatility and sustaining public expenditure in periods of revenue shortfalls (Stabilisation Fund). The remaining share is channelled to the national budget through the Annual Budget Funding Amount and shall serve for spending and investment in priority sectors such as agriculture, education, health and infrastructure. However, since the discovery of the Jubilee field, subsequent offshore discoveries, specifically the Twenboa-Enyenra-Ntomme and Offshore Cape Three Points fields, have increased Ghana's estimated reserves to between 5 and 7 billion barrels. This suggests that Ghana's production time horizon may be longer than initially expected. Assuming these additional reserves prove real and can be developed, the rationale for saving more now for future generations is reduced. Reducing the rationale further is the growing debt of Ghana. From 2006 to 2016, government debt increased from 30% of GDP to over 70%[3] with aggregate borrowings costs estimated to be 4.1% on external debt.[4] Yet, the return on the Ghana Heritage Fund in 2016 was 1.79%.[5] Such a difference calls into question the rationale of accumulating long-term savings, rather than reducing government debt, unless the return on those savings is greater than the country's borrowing costs.

For countries where there is ample capital and where resource revenues are long lasting, the priority should be on managing volatility and achieving macro-fiscal stability. Countries in this situation are Saudi Arabia, Kuwait and other Gulf Cooperation Council countries. These countries have funds that provide a stabilisation and savings function.

For countries where capital is scarce and where resource revenues are long lasting, the priority should be to invest revenues domestically, while accounting for absorptive capacity constraints and maintaining macroeconomic stability. A country in this situation is Nigeria, which funnels resource revenues through the budget, where spending is based on a benchmark oil price and where surpluses go into the Excess Crude Account.[6] The latter was set up in 2004 to stabilise oil revenues. Kazakhstan fits partly into this category. The economy's existing capital stock is dominated by the extractive sectors, which have been successful at attracting FDI. The challenge going forward for Kazakhstan is developing and attracting greater investments to its non-resource sectors.[7]

Prioritising development without earmarking natural resource revenues

Parallel to the saving versus spending trade-off dilemma is how to ensure the spending of natural resource revenues improves development outcomes. Some countries have utilised strict earmarking practices to channel natural resource revenues to particular budget items. However, earmarking generally reduces fiscal flexibility and is open to capture from special interests, leading to underinvestment or overinvestment (see Box 2.3). As the cases of **Botswana** and **Indonesia** show, earmarking is not necessary to ensure that non-renewable resource revenues are invested in physical and human capital in support of sustainable socio-economic development.

Botswana notionally earmarks resource revenues for this goal, without relying on strict statutory expenditure requirements. It is simply a commitment to development policy that the government of Botswana and its parliament have stood by. This commitment can be seen in the progress Botswana has made in terms of development since independence. In Indonesia, the oil windfall of the 1970s helped to scale and expand a development agenda that had preceded the unexpected revenue windfall. The economic diversification that followed and the government's efforts to minimise the macroeconomic impact and fiscal policy dependence on hydrocarbon revenues buffered the economy once oil prices declined in the 1980s. Both countries successfully combined sound macroeconomic management with clear long-term development policies.

In comparison to many other resource-rich developing countries, Botswana is frequently considered an economic success story and a model for others to follow in the prudent management of natural resource revenues. Botswana has had continuous civilian rule since declaring independence from Britain in 1966 and is one of the longest-running multiparty democracies in Africa. When the country declared independence, there were only 12 kilometres of paved road and most of the population did not have secondary education (Acemoglu, Johnson and Robinson, 2002). Yet, from independence to the late 1990s, Botswana was one of the fastest growing economies in the world, comparable only to China, with average annual growth of 10%. As a result, Botswana has developed from one of the poorest countries to achieve upper middle-income status in a generation. Poverty has also reduced considerably. In 1985, 59% of the population lived in poverty. As of 2009, only 19.3% live in poverty.[8]

While non-violent political stability and sound institutions have underpinned Botswana's growth and development, the country's large diamond deposits have also been a crucial factor. Between 1985-1994, the mining sector declined from 42.2% of GDP to 22.2% of GDP as a result of economic diversification policies. However, the country is still reliant on the diamond trade, with the mining sector providing a significant source of income to the government. But this has also declined: between 1985-1994, 50.9% of government income came from the sector. Between 2004-14 mining income represented 39.9% of government revenues.

Botswana's natural resource revenue management framework rests on two pillars: macroeconomic stability and the prioritisation of development expenditure. These two pillars are operationalised through the Sustainable Budget Index and the Pula Fund, a stabilisation and savings fund.[9] Public spending in Botswana is based on an annual budget process and informed by National Development Plans (NDP). The NDPs, which cover periods of six years, outline broad strategic development priorities that the government intends to achieve during the period, as well as specific development projects that will be supported. The expenditure framework follows the principle that *natural resource revenues should only be used to finance investment in assets that maintain the country's current asset base or improve the asset base for future income generation* as mining revenues decrease over time. This implies that natural resource revenues should finance investment (outlined in the NDPs) in physical assets, namely electricity, water and roads, as well as investments in human capital, namely in education, training and health. The corollary is that non-mineral revenues finance recurrent expenditure. This principle is operationalised through the Sustainable Budget Index (SBI), which is defined as the ratio of non-investment spending to non-mineral revenues. An SBI of 1 signifies that non-investment expenditure is financed partly by mineral revenues. An SBI less than 1 implies that non-mineral revenue is financing recurrent expenditure whereas mineral revenue is financing investment and/or is being saved (in the Pula Fund). Since fiscal year 1983/84, the SBI has been below one, save for the period 2001-05 when the SBI was over one. In calculating the SBI, it should be noted that education and health, which would normally be accounted for as recurrent expenditure because the majority of spending is allocated to the salaries of teachers and medical professionals, are classified as investment expenditure.

Botswana is, in effect, notionally earmarking revenues from mineral production for socioeconomic development by using the SBI. However, this is not a pure form of on-budget earmarking. Mineral revenues are not institutionally segregated from the budget but consolidated with other government receipts. However, there is no statutory basis for the SBI. It is not an ex-ante rule that policy makers must abide by in determining the budget allocation. The SBI is rather a principle which guides expenditure and savings decision making in relation to the broader development policy outlined in the NDPs. Ultimately, this framework relies on the principled commitment of the parliament and the executive in the drafting and approval of the budget and the development policies therein. Given that the SBI is not an ex-ante rule, there is flexibility in the budget-setting process. As such, Botswana avoids the budget constraints that conventional earmarking can bring. At the same time, the Pula Fund provides an important stabilisation function to ensure that this development expenditure does not succumb to absorptive capacity constraints and negative Dutch disease effects. The accumulated savings in the Pula Fund may, in turn, support continued development expenditure for future generations.

Box 2.3. The pitfalls of earmarking natural resource revenues

Earmarking is a common practice in public finance in developed and developing countries, including the earmarking of natural resource revenues. One justification for earmarking is the so-called benefit principle, whereby a tax is levied on a specific activity to pay for that activity (e.g. fuel taxes to finance road construction and maintenance). By this logic, there is a strong link between the beneficiary and the liability. The earmarking of natural resource revenues does not, in most cases, have a strong link. Notwithstanding, earmarking of natural resource revenues for various purposes is practised among some natural resource-rich countries. Motivations for earmarking non-renewable resource revenues include drawing public attention to their use, protecting spending on socio-economic development priorities and discouraging expenditure on recurrent budget items, and ensuring an equitable distribution across subnational regions.

While the motivations for earmarking of non-renewable resource revenues may seem sound, the evidence of their effectiveness is mixed, and in some cases (e.g. Venezuela) highly negative. There are several disadvantages to earmarking. It can constrain budgetary flexibility. It may lead to government inefficiency, and overinvestment or underinvestment in certain public services. It may also contribute to procyclicality of public expenditure. Furthermore, earmarking, in some cases, has been fashioned such that it is not subject to parliamentary oversight. This may undermine public financial management and public investment.

Ecuador has had a history of extensively earmarking oil revenues, which has led to significant budget inflexibility without resulting in better fiscal and policy outcomes. The budget process in Ecuador has been characterised by multiple competing interest groups, institutional instability and limited incentives for long-term co-operation. Consequently, periods of higher oil revenues have led to rent-seeking behaviour in the form of increased discretionary spending or earmarking of allocations to different groups, such as subnational governments or specific budget items (Acosta Mejía, Albornoz, and Caridad Araujo, 2009). As a 2006 study by Almeida, Gallardo and Tomaselli (2006) determined, 92% of the central government's budget was inflexible, meaning that most income was already assigned to specific spending targets, guaranteed subsidies and debt repayments. This left the central government with little room for fiscal adjustment.

Paradoxically, the Ecuadorian government had moved toward fiscal consolidation and rationalisation in the late 1990s. Between 2000 and 2006, Ecuador established five natural resource funds to support stabilisation and savings. This effort did not lead to greater rationalisation or flexibility in public financial management of oil revenues (Cueva and Ortiz, 2013). Although the funds provided some element of stabilisation and savings, they did not operate as conventional stabilisation and savings funds. Rather, they were vehicles for earmarking oil revenues to different projects. From 1999 to 2006 the oil funds received approximately USD 6.2 billion. Of this amount 79% was spent. Of the remaining USD 1.4 billion at the end of 2007, much of the funds were used to compensate the difference between the budgeted oil price and the effective price. Nearly a quarter of the funds were used to repay government debt, and 16% was invested in the energy sector. As Cueva and Ortiz (2013, 10) argue, all of the funds had stabilisation as one of their objectives. However, additional mandates and

> the complicated, confusing, and opaque on-budget and off-budget earmarking schemes rendered the stabilisation mechanism ineffective. Moreover, the complexity of the earmarking, and when and how deposits were made, constrained government's ability to prioritise spending efficiently. As Lopez-Murphy et al. (2010) find, earmarking exacerbated spending pressures during the 2003-08 oil boom.
>
> In 2008, a constitutional assembly was called, which eliminated all the oil funds and all oil revenue earmarking schemes, recentralising and rationalising the allocation and management of oil revenues. One reason given for dismantling the system was that the schemes favoured debt repayment rather than social spending. This effort was furthered by the introduction of a single point for collecting oil revenues, the Single Treasury Account, which is part of the budget (Arrellano-Yanguas and Mejía Acosta, 2014).

During the two oil booms of the 1970s, Indonesia mobilised the oil windfall to advance major investments in education provision across the country, while also channelling the windfall to economic diversification projects. Indonesia was the most populous and the poorest of the countries in the world to receive an oil windfall. In 1974, GDP per capita was USD 200. However, the country did not earmark oil revenues to specific expenditures; oil revenues accrued to the central government budget. However, as oil revenues provided the majority of the government budget during the period, it can be interpreted as a case of symbolic earmarking. Oil revenues peaked at more than 70% of the budget in the early 1980s, falling to roughly 20% by the mid-1990s (Alisjahbana, 2005). Development spending doubled because of the oil windfall. In 1973, development expenditure was 63% the amount spent on current expenditures. By 1975, development expenditure exceeded current expenditure by 25%. Development expenditure either matched or exceeded current expenditure through the remainder of the oil boom (Gelb, 1988).

Some of this increased development expenditure was channelled to the Sekolah Dasar (basic education) programme. Between 1973 and 1979, Indonesia constructed 61 807 schools. This was the world's largest ever school construction programme (1.5% of 1973 GDP). The number of schools built represented 1 for every 500 children aged 5-14 in 1971. Each school was designed for 120 students and 3 teachers. The central government also recruited and paid the teachers' salaries. Enrolment of children aged 7 to 12 increased from 69% to 83%. Before the programme in the early 1970s, enrolment had been declining and there was no capital investment in schools. Duflo (2001) estimates that the programme led to an average increase of 0.12 to 0.19 years of education, with an increase in wages of 1.5% to 2.7%. This suggests that the large government intervention in the supply of education was effective. As such, Indonesia made efficient use of the oil windfall.

Indonesia also employed the oil windfall to advance agricultural development. Major investments were made in developing natural gas resources, for export to Japan and as an input for agricultural fertiliser production. Fertiliser was then distributed to farmers at subsidised prices, a practice which continues currently. With the benefit of new high-yield and disease-resistant rice varieties, Indonesia farmers greatly increased yields, pushing down prices for consumers. As a predominantly rural and agricultural-based economy, improved agricultural production and lower prices helped support economic diversification, underwriting the movement and growth of labour to low-wage export-orientated manufacturing in the early 1980s. Rural economies were furthermore supported by major investments in infrastructure (including construction of schools for the *Sekolah Dasar* programme), receiving a quarter of public infrastructure investment during the oil boom.

The lesson to draw from Indonesia is that this prioritisation of development expenditure did not require a specific earmarking of oil revenues. In fact, these development policy priorities had been established before the oil boom, which came unexpectedly. The oil boom simply facilitated the large-scale expansion and rollout of these programmes (Gelb, 2012). During the oil booms of the 1970s, the government operated with a formal balanced budget rule. Bureaucratic controls were also applied, though without much public transparency, to slow public expenditure. Consequently, the country achieved a fiscal surplus and doubled its international reserves. When oil prices fell in the early 1980s, the government, which was not constrained by specific earmarks, quickly adjusted fiscal policy, scaling back planned projects and restructuring public spending. The investments made in physical and human capital development during the boom provided a cushion to support economic growth in the non-extractives sectors, helped additionally by an exchange rate policy that limited real exchange rate appreciation and progressive trade and FDI liberalisation. By 2005, manufacturing represented 47% of merchandise exports, which is significant for a country with a large and diverse natural resource endowment.

Assessing direct distribution mechanisms

Proponents of direct distribution cash transfers in the context of distributing natural resource revenues contend that by distributing resource revenues directly to citizens, cash transfer mechanisms have the potential to advance sustainable development outcomes more effectively than through more conventional revenue distribution methods, such as annual budget processes. By addressing the tendency for wealth appropriation by elites, for example, and encouraging public oversight, cash transfers may also mitigate the impact of resource revenues on governance. Providing a population with a sense of ownership over a portion of the profits garnered from natural resource extraction, is likely to encourage engagement through the development of a political constituency with an interest in managing revenues well, with positive implications for transparency, institutional integrity and governance. Noting the role of taxation in building accountability between the state and its citizens, Moss, Lambert and Majerowicz (2015) and others have also argued that this contract is strengthened if the transfers are also taxed. That is, by providing each citizen the right to a dividend of their country's resource wealth, and then taxing that dividend, cash transfers may create an incentive to counter the erosion of the social contract by the fiscal autonomy provided by large resource rents.

Given the volatility of natural resource revenues and absorptive capacity constraints, there is strong evidence to suggest that any consideration of direct distribution through cash transfers should aim first to complement fiscal policy objectives that support macroeconomic stability, namely through the establishment of a stabilisation fund (Gupta, Segura-Ubiergo and Flores, 2014). Discussions on the advantages and disadvantages of cash transfers are not separate from efforts to establish a macroeconomic framework that seeks to smooth out revenue volatility, while dealing with resource exhaustibility issues. While allocating resource revenues directly to citizens may reduce poverty and improve natural resource revenue accountability, there is an opportunity cost. Supporting a cash-transfer mechanism may take away from other productivity-improving public expenditure and investment, such as in infrastructure, healthcare and education.

Effective implementation of a direct distribution cash transfer programme also depends on the government's administrative capacity. This includes ensuring the verification of identity as well as the actual transfer of funds. Many developing countries face the challenge of financial exclusion, where the poor have limited or no access to the banking sector, particularly in rural areas. The administrative burden of implementing a cash transfer programme may prove prohibitive to some countries lacking the necessary infrastructure and administrative capacity or may allow for leakages and misuse. Technological developments, such as mobile money (for example, M-PESA in Kenya), alternative currencies and phone banking, have increased the availability of banking services to the poor and can provide a means to overcome this challenge.[10] Brazil's *Bolsa Familia*, for example – a conditional cash transfer programme that provides 12 million families with monthly stipends if children regularly attend school and are vaccinated – is administered through electronic payments, helping to reduce administrative costs, while biometric and other identification systems may help to eliminate leakages, misuse and other inefficiencies.

A further concern expressed in the literature on both direct distribution cash transfers and conditional cash transfer programmes is reduction of work incentives. Some have argued that if individuals receive income outside a framework of remuneration for work, it will have a negative effect on productivity and employment, and therefore the competitiveness of the non-resource sector (Isakova, Plekhanov and Zettelmeyer, 2012). The evidence on this is mixed, suggesting that transfers are unlikely to create disincentives to work if they are not conditional on income or employment, that is, if they are universal, and also are not too large in size. In Alaska, for example, a survey conducted after the launch of the Permanent Fund Dividend scheme reported that only 1% of respondents claimed to have started working less because of the dividend (Knapp et al., 1984). Further, programme design decisions relating to the size or proportion of total revenues to distribute as a cash transfer could overcome this risk by capping transfers (Moss, Lambert and Majerowicz, 2015, 15). Providing a regular cash transfer can support the poorest in terms of maximising welfare, with the evidence suggesting that cash transfer programmes lead to increased individual spending on health, nutrition and education (Yanez-Pagans, 2008).

Further work is also required to implement high quality monitoring and evaluation systems of those conditional cash transfer programmes already in place. Monitoring and evaluation of cash transfer programmes currently varies significantly across regions and models. In some cases, such as Bangladesh, implementation has also suggested that cash transfers are only likely to have a positive development outcome when any increase in demand for services is met by sufficient supply (Arnold, Conway and Greenslade, 2011). Different implementation choices may therefore need to be considered in low- and middle-income contexts, where there is a lower level of development in terms of services. There is also the possibility that cash transfers may not treat deeper causes of inequality, such as divergence in skills and changing economic environments. In the case of Mongolia, despite increased revenues, public spending on education declined as a share of GDP between 2002 and 2009, from 7.9% to 5.6% (Isakova, Plekhanov and Zettelmeyer, 2012, 15). The demand for services that may result from a cash transfer programme should be matched therefore by relevant complementary investments.

Multiple design and implementation decisions must therefore be measured when considering direct distribution cash transfer mechanisms as a means of natural resource revenue distribution. Design choices concern the value (including, for example, whether all or just a portion of resource revenues are distributed through a cash transfer mechanism), the duration and frequency of transfers, as well as their coverage. That is, whether payments should be universal, targeted, or governed or limited by any kind of conditionality. Implementation questions include a country's capacity for administration and monitoring, and the choice of payment mechanisms such as electronic payment systems, to reduce costs and leakage while also promoting inclusion.

Other considerations include the kinds of parallel steps that need to be taken to make the programme successful and to ensure that a cash transfer programme forms part of an overarching, fiscal and economic policy approach that supports macroeconomic stability and long-term economic development. If, for example, the cash transfer mechanism exists without concomitant stabilisation mechanisms (e.g. stabilisation and savings fund) to manage the volatility of natural resource revenues over time, the cash transfer mechanism will mirror that volatility (see Box 2.4). The cash transfer would be less reliable, and it would be pro-cyclical. The utility of the cash transfer may also be less in an unstable economic environment, as citizens have less confidence in the expected outcomes of their consumption and savings decision. Citizens may identify individually rational spending and savings opportunities, but failing systemic improvements in development across the economy, these opportunities may be highly constrained or limited.[11]

A number of resource-rich developing countries have implemented cash transfer programmes in the context of managing windfall revenues for the purposes of achieving development goals. **Timor-Leste**, for example, started collecting substantial oil revenues in 2005, and shortly thereafter established the Petroleum Fund (PF).[12] The revenues obtained from oil and gas extraction have been key to Timor-Leste's post-independence reconstruction and development.[13] As revenues became several times larger than the country's pre-oil economy, spending dramatically increased between 2004 and 2009 and the Government determined to use the income derived from the exploitation of oil and gas resources to establish mandatory financial reserve. To achieve this, the PF Law, administered by the Timor-Leste Ministry of Planning and Finance, required that all petroleum revenues be transferred to the Fund and invested in foreign financial assets. The Fund's only outgoings were transfers back to the central government budget, contingent on parliamentary approval. According to the legislation, up to 3% of the net value of the country's oil resources were to be transferred to the budget in any year, but further withdrawals could be justified by the executive and approved by parliament.

Although spending included large infrastructure projects and public contracts, an extensive cash transfer programme was also implemented in 2008. Rather than being linked to the PF, however, cash transfers were financed directly from the general budget (Moss, Lambert and Majerowicz, 2015, 59). The transfers were also not universal, but were used primarily to promote stability or to meet social protection objectives. The first transfers in 2008 were primarily distributed to veterans of the 24-year struggle for independence from Indonesia. At the same time, one-off cash grants were also made to a group of disgruntled soldiers known as "petitioners," others to the elderly, while another programme targeted vulnerable, low-income households headed by women (Moss, Lambert and Majerowicz, 2015, 66). Unlike the Alaska model,

Timor-Leste did not link cash transfers to the fund, but instead used its increased budget capacity to fund social protection and post-conflict stability policies. As such, despite being triggered by increased spending capacity provided by natural resource revenues, the Timor-Leste programmes are closer to a conditional cash transfer programme, and not a direct distribution mechanism of natural resource revenues or the income of a savings fund. Rather, they are social programmes that form part of the budget process. What is key is that the framework for managing natural resource revenues in Timor-Leste provides budgetary stability over time such that these policies can be implemented sustainably.

Targeted cash transfer programmes may also provide an effective means to reform fossil fuel subsidies, which have proven very difficult to reform in many countries. For example, India's cooking gas subsidy programme is the largest direct benefit cash transfer programme in the world. In contrast to a system of price subsidies, the programme makes direct payments to beneficiaries' bank accounts to support the purchase of cooking gas. Available evidence suggests that the programme has reduced leakages and diversions of cooking gas to the commercial market. As such, the programme works directly for genuine beneficiaries. The cooking gas subsidy programme also makes use of India's biometric ID system, which eliminates duplication of beneficiaries and improves access to the poor and rural beneficiaries, particularly women.[14]

Box 2.4. Mongolia's experience with resources-to-cash

Like other developing countries rich in natural resources, Mongolia has also faced the challenge of balancing the need to save for the future while addressing the needs of the short term. Following adoption of the National Development Strategy by Parliament in 2008, the Mongolian legislature established in November 2009 the Human Development Fund, with the goal of providing every citizen a portion of the country's mineral wealth (Campi, 2012). By law the Fund was to be financed from mining revenues received by the state and from a portion of royalty payments, the value of which was not specified in the legislation (Isakova, Plekhanov and Zettelmeyer, 2012, 11). According to the legislation, these funds could be used for cash payments to all citizens, as well as for social payments addressing pensions, healthcare, universal child grants, education and housing. The law did not stipulate the size of the payments; rather, the revenues and expenditures of the fund were to be determined as part of the annual budget process.

In 2009, the Parliament also passed a law (based on similar legislation in Chile) creating a mechanism for saving surplus revenue from mineral royalties in order to stabilise the annual budget when mineral prices fell, as in 2008. While this subsequently formed the basis of the Fund's capital, the first contribution to the Fund came from royalties from the Oyu Tolgoi project, leading in February 2010 to every citizen receiving a cash transfer of MNT 70 000 (approximately USD 50, or 2% of per capita GDP), followed shortly thereafter by further smaller payments. Public promises spurred by the election cycle were made to make total annual cash transfers of MNT 1.5 million per capita (approximately USD 1 200, or almost half of per capita GDP). In 2011, monthly cash transfers were made of MNT 21 000, leading to projected annual spending on cash payments of around 10% of the 2010 GDP.

> Mongolia's cash transfer programme quickly burdened the state's budget (Yeung and Howes, 2015). Following a balance of payment crisis and subsequent IMF bailout in 2010, the Parliament adopted a set of fiscal rules (the Fiscal Stability Law) to set ceilings on expenditure growth, structural budget deficits and on government debt. When commodity prices fell again, Mongolia was forced again to seek further support from the IMF. In 2012, further laws were subsequently introduced to limit budget deficits to 2% of GDP, and shortly thereafter, the cash payments were reformed from ad hoc payments to regular dividends (Moss, Lambert, and Majerowicz 2015, 59). The Mongolian government also considered around this time listing the shares of the state-owned company that holds the Tavan Tolgoi licence and parts of its development rights. While this never eventuated, a portion of the shares would have been distributed equally to the population, entitling holders to a flow of dividends, and therefore linking payments to the performance of management of commodity revenues (Isakova, Plekhanov and Zettelmeyer, 2012, 23).
>
> Despite several measures seeking to stabilise the fiscal environment, Mongolia's cash transfer programme was unsustainable and may have contributed negatively to the country's fiscal and budgetary troubles. As of February 2016, the government passed a law establishing a new sovereign wealth fund, the Future Heritage Fund, to accumulate a proportion of natural resource revenues and to promote medium- and long-term fiscal stability considering the ongoing volatility in commodity prices. The fund aimed to save 20% of mineral revenues in any given year and was to absorb the indebted fund for cash transfers.
>
> Mongolia did not link the payment of cash transfers to the performance of the fund, and neither mine site was generating 10% of GDP in revenues when spending at that rate on cash transfers peaked. As a result, the cash transfer programme undercut the accumulation of assets in the Fund. This also undermined the programme's capacity to incentivise good governance by contributing to a sense of public ownership over the management of the assets, and thus for the cash transfer programme to strengthen incentives in the resource sector through increased public oversight. The Mongolia case also highlights the potential for cash transfers to contribute to inflationary pressure in an economy with weak absorptive capacity. In Mongolia, the first cash transfer took place during a winter that saw a major loss of livestock, which the European Bank for Reconstruction and Development notes contributed to a marked acceleration in inflation, from 6% to around 12% (Isakova, Plekhanov and Zettelmeyer, 2012).
>
> The Development Bank of Mongolia, created in May 2011, also had the possibility of accessing the Human Development Fund for social housing and infrastructure projects at the request of cabinet. This suggests a series of design and implementation decisions that undermined Mongolia's cash transfer programme as an effective means of revenue distribution and a driver of inclusive development.

Strategic investment funds as emerging tools for extra-budgetary investment

Relying on any one sector entails significant risk for the economy if that industry underperforms. Diversification is particularly important for natural resource producing countries, as diversification of the economy is another means of providing stability to the economy in face of the potentially extreme volatility of natural resource prices and revenues. A more diverse economy, in principle, can better weather a downturn in natural resource revenues. This is true for any economy that relies so heavily on a single or a few industries. As such, some resource-rich countries are establishing strategic investment funds geared toward fostering economic diversification by catalysing new sectors in the economy and making investments in infrastructure and R&D capabilities to support long-term growth and economic competitiveness.[15] Hence, strategic investment funds are a possible means for natural resource-rich countries to ensure efficient and sound extra-budgetary investment decisions. As strategic investment funds operate with a double bottom-line objective, this can help resource-rich countries better scrutinise the financial and economic feasibility of development-oriented projects and avoid wasting resources on so-called white elephant projects.

A key characteristic of strategic investment funds is that they adopt the organisational and operational practices of similar types of investment funds operating in the private sector (e.g. private equity; venture capital). The aim is to bring the investment tools and practices used by comparable investment funds in the private sector to a public-sector entity. Moreover, strategic investment funds follow a double bottom-line logic: the aim is to generate financial returns as well as positive returns for socio-economic development. In effect, strategic investment funds are a tool for government to utilise or capitalise on private-sector capabilities and resources, in this instance the investment practices and standards of similar types of funds operating in the private sector, to kick-start and drive productive growth and development.

Strategic investment funds are not, however, a replacement for conventional modes of public investment and expenditure via the budget. Rather, strategic investment funds are a complementary tool that government can utilise to deploy capital within the economy. Yet, as a tool for government and given their combined financial and development remit, strategic investment funds are most effective as part of a broader policy and institutional development and reform pathway.[16]

Strategic investment funds are also different from sovereign wealth funds that have a domestic investment mandate or have been used to finance domestic projects outside of the government budget. This residual category of sovereign wealth fund, which is atypical, is not covered in this report.[17] Strategic investment funds are likewise distinct from national development banks, although they may have similar development objectives. A key difference between a strategic investment fund and a national development bank is that a development bank may be more likely to fund projects that produce below market returns (Gelb et al., 2014). The activities of national development banks are also not covered in this report.

Strategic investment funds are typically established with start-up capital financed by the state budget (or some other form of government revenue or savings). The decision to establish and finance such funds is thus subject both to state financing and parliamentary (or executive) scrutiny at the outset. However, strategic investment funds are typically established as autonomous entities with investment decision making made independently of direct government influence. They are rarely accounted for in the state budget and can thus be classified as extra-budgetary entities.[18] However, their performance and adherence to their intended objective(s) is still subject to periodic government review.[19]

The investment practices used by strategic investment funds are wide-ranging. Evidence shows that many strategic investment funds invest in different parts of the capital structure of firms (i.e. debt and equity) and large infrastructure projects.

Investments are made in large but also small and medium-sized enterprises, and in infrastructure for example. They are also investors in private equity funds but also venture capital funds. Strategic investment funds take minority equity stakes and in some case majority equity stakes. Some strategic investment funds also use leverage to increase their capital under management. Finally, many strategic investment funds, such as the Russian Direct Investment Fund (see Box 2.5), seek to co-invest with external investors at home and abroad, to leverage capital investments but also to access a qualified and credible cadre of skills and expertise.

Some strategic investment funds are holding companies of state-owned enterprises and other real assets. In contrast with a simple holding company, the strategic investment fund exercises its ownership rights by demanding better performance of these assets.[20] On the one hand, the fund is motivated to maximise its financial performance. On the other hand, as a strategic investor, the fund is motivated to improve productivity and outcomes at the level of the national economy; and particularly in relation to state-owned entities or firms. Reinforcing activity could include pressing for changes to corporate governance and operational practices to move these firms closer to practices in the private sector. While aiming to improve financial performance, this reinforcing strategy is also a precursor to partial or complete privatisation of these assets. This strategy is not about supporting poorly performing state assets that are unlikely to show growth in the future. Rather, the strategy aims to improve the performance of state assets that show potential.

Senegal is an example of a country attempting to catalyse new economic opportunities via a strategic investment fund. At the end of 2012 the National Assembly of Senegal passed legislation establishing the Fonds Souverains d'Investissements Stratégiques (FONSIS), with operations officially launched in October 2013. FONSIS is modelling itself on Singapore's Temasek. The goal is to consolidate and reinforce the government's existing holdings, while making new investments alongside partners in the private sector to increase the productivity and dynamism of the economy.[21] FONSIS is focusing initially on investments in Senegal, but its founding legislation allows for investments to be made abroad.

One area FONSIS has been crucial in kick-starting is solar power production. In 2016 work began on the construction of the Senergy Project, a 30-megawatt solar power plant. With production expected to begin in 2017, the Senergy Project will be West Africa's largest photovoltaic power facility. While providing renewable energy to Senegal, the project adds more diversity to Senegal's energy mix. Senergy is co-financed by EUR 43 million in capital from FONSIS, Paris-based investment fund Méridiam, which focuses on the preparation and delivery of long-term public infrastructure projects, and PROPARCO, a subsidiary of the French Development Agency. Although FONSIS is a new organisation, and the work on the Senergy Project has just begun, the development of the Project itself signals its potential as a strategic investment fund in catalysing new economic opportunities for Senegal.

Box 2.5. Collaboration and co-investment in Russia

Strategic investment funds are often geared towards attracting co-investors. The strategic investment fund may help support the privatisation of state-owned assets. But it may also act as an anchor investor for other firms going public, buying a large equity stake to ensure a successful initial public offering that attracts other external investors. Or, it may attract other co-investors to partner on private equity transactions. Outside capital or co-investment opportunities can be generated by the fund due to its unique position of understanding of local economic opportunities and conditions. Ultimately, the aim is to increase foreign investment in the economy, with the strategic investment fund being one platform for doing so.

An early trendsetter in collaboration and co-investment has been the Russia Direct Investment Fund. In 2011 the Russian government embarked on a new strategy for attracting foreign direct investment by establishing the Russia Direct Investment Fund (RDIF) with USD 10 billion of committed capital. This new strategic investment fund was established expressly as a co-investment vehicle, with the objective of supporting economic modernisation of the Russian economy by investing in high growth Russian companies and essential infrastructure. Making co-investment a core strategy of the fund made it unique among other sovereign investors at the time, with many now following this trend.

For foreign investors, many of them sovereign wealth funds, the RDIF provided a platform for investing in Russia. RDIF's selling point is that it has a deep understanding of the local economy and local investment opportunities. Given its intent to foment economic modernisation of the Russian economy, the fund's investment focus is on investing in high growth Russian companies, sectors where Russia has a sustainable competitive advantage, and where there are opportunities to increase significantly the efficiency of Russian producers.

Since its inception, the proportion of RDIF capital to funds of foreign investment partners has been 10 to 1. RDIF has closed more than 30 deals across different sectors in the economy with more than 20 partnerships it has formed with other sovereign investors, such as Abu Dhabi's Mubadala, Bahrain's Mumtalakat, the China Investment Corporation, and private-sector investment funds.

Investments have been made in major infrastructure projects, such as modernising the Russian energy grid and building a railway bridge over the Amur river connecting Russia with China. China also co-invested with RDIF in a large stake in Russia's second largest wood processing company, RFP Group. Other investments include RDIF acting as an anchor investor to co-investors to the initial public offering of MD Medical Group, Russia's leading private network of prenatal clinics and hospitals. This investment helped to increase access to higher quality medical care in Russia's regions, by building modern medical centres, developing training opportunities for healthcare specialists, and introducing international technological and safety standards.

Although RDIF has made considerable progress as a co-investment platform, many partnerships have not progressed beyond the commitment stage due to the economic sanctions adversely affecting RDIF's ability to attract capital. Notwithstanding, RDIF's commitment to building co-investment opportunities and its proven capacity to attract investment partners before sanctions shows that it is an effective organisation and a potentially attractive model for other countries to emulate.

A key challenge for the strategic investment fund is the need at some level to co-ordinate across government to avoid duplication of public investment, while still remaining independent from political influence. The most obvious case in which this occurs is when investing in public goods such as infrastructure, where the fund can act as an interface between government and the private sector. It is unlikely to occur, and unnecessary, when the fund is making investments in private-sector companies. Co-ordination should not lead, moreover, to a reduction in the independence of the fund. While many strategic investment funds are operationally independent from government, it is important to maintain some degree of co-ordination (and awareness) with other public investment programmes. There is a risk that the independent operation of these funds could undermine the quality of other public investment programmes, where similar and overlapping objectives exist. Absent or insufficient co-ordination can result in the fragmented and inefficient use of public funds (Allen and Tommasi, 2001; Allen and Radev, 2010). Such concerns may, however, be attenuated with an appropriate governance architecture and clear alignment with wider macroeconomic and fiscal policy. Nigeria is an example of a country working in this direction.

In 2011, Nigeria established the Nigeria Sovereign Investment Authority (NSIA) as an independent agency to manage the country's new sovereign wealth fund. Although initially seeded with just USD 1 billion in operating capital to manage roughly 0.25% of GDP, the founding of the NSIA represented the beginnings of a new direction in the country's natural resource revenue management. The NSIA was given three objectives: establish a savings base for the Nigerian people; enhance the development of Nigerian infrastructure; and provide stabilisation support in times of economic stress. Within the NSIA there are, as such, three separate funds: the Future Generations fund, the Stabilisation Fund and the Nigeria Infrastructure Fund. While the savings and stabilisation portfolios are invested abroad, the Nigeria Infrastructure Fund takes the form of a strategic investment fund that can invest domestically on a commercial basis and with the aim of generating a financial return, and preferably via co-investments with external investors. However, this does not mean that it makes infrastructure investments without consideration of other public sector priorities for essential infrastructure development. But it does have independent discretion over the projects in which it chooses to invest.

The Nigeria Infrastructure Fund each year develops a Five-Year Infrastructure Investment rolling plan. What area of infrastructure is open to investment is unlimited, so long as it stimulates growth and diversification of the Nigerian economy. However, the fund has prioritised sectors that have the potential for nation-wide economic impact, that have attractive social and commercial returns, have a conducive regulatory environment, and a capacity to attract further private-sector (and other sovereign wealth fund) participation in the investment. The current focus is on healthcare infrastructure, real estate (particularly mass affordable housing), motorways, and power generation. These areas were chosen in consultation with relevant government ministries and regulatory agencies, as well as sector experts. And, in some cases, a strategic partnership is formed. In healthcare, for example, the NSIA is part of strategic partnership agreements with the Federal Ministry of Health with the aim of identifying healthcare infrastructure projects with leading global healthcare sector participants. In agriculture, the NSIA is one of three sponsors of the Fund for Agriculture Finance in Nigeria, along with the Nigerian Federal Ministry of Agriculture and Rural Development and the German government-owned KfW development bank. Both examples show that although NSIA is independent, it co-ordinates with other parts of government. Importantly, including an external partner multiplies the investment and provides greater scrutiny and due diligence of any deal.

Although there are longer running experiences to draw from (e.g. Singapore; Malaysia), the use of strategic investment funds is relatively new. Moreover, their use in developing countries is limited save for a few cases. However, early experiences (e.g. Senegal and Nigeria) suggest that the quality and effectiveness of a strategic investment fund depends on its ability to balance and measure its dual functions; to establish a clear threshold for risks which is amendable to adjustments when there is a need to change track; and to account for its investment governance such that the organisation can operate and execute its strategic investment mandate following clear commercial principles and without unwarranted political interference. This does not mean that strategic investment funds are not accountable to government for their performance and their adherence to their dual mandate. As such, strategic investments funds should follow accepted standards of disclosure and transparency, signalling to their domestic and international stakeholders their commitment to the strategic development mission and their commercial orientation.

3. Key policy recommendations

Non-renewable natural resource revenues can make an important contribution to harnessing inclusive growth and sustainable development, provided that resource revenues are appropriately managed to smooth revenue flows throughout the price cycle and effectively spent domestically to transform natural resource revenues into productive development gains. In order to translate finite assets into productive and long-lasting development gains policy makers need to address two main challenges and consider the following recommended policy responses.

Policy Challenge 1: How to reconcile long-term development and intergenerational equity objectives with the need to manage the volatility and uncertainty of exhaustible resource revenues.

Recommended policy responses:

- *Policy makers need to adopt a clear and consistent fiscal policy and macroeconomic management framework* that counters price volatility and helps to insulate the economy from price, production or other external shocks, while smoothing public expenditures over time in support of the achievement of long-term development objectives.

- *Policy makers need to ensure budget stability and fiscal sustainability over time, including through the establishment, where appropriate, of properly sized stabilisation and savings funds as an integral part of the fiscal policy and macroeconomic management framework.* "Where appropriate" refers to resource-dependent countries whose economies are highly correlated with commodity price volatility and who stand to benefit from the financial buffers offered by stabilisation funds. Establishing a framework for managing natural resource revenues including a stabilisation fund should occur before the commencement of production, or as soon as possible thereafter. This includes countries that have revenues from existing production. As a source of precautionary savings, stabilisation funds should be invested in safe foreign assets to ensure sufficient liquidity to counter price volatility. Stabilisation funds provide consistency in government expenditure and planning. They can also provide an insurance against unexpected negative economic shocks, giving the government extra resources at a time of need. Stabilisation funds are not effective vehicles for helping satisfy domestic capital needs, particularly in capital-starved developing economies where domestic assets are likely to be highly correlated with commodity prices given the structure of resource-dependent economies. Arbitrary withdrawals and manipulation of withdrawal rules must be avoided to prevent undermining the stabilisation policy objective and therefore reproducing the volatility of the natural resource revenues that the stabilisation fund has been tasked with eliminating. This safeguards the capacity of the fund as a renewable financial resource that can be called upon when needed under the auspices of the withdrawal rules and procedures. Savings funds provide a longer-term renewable financial resource once the natural resources no longer provide the income they once did. However, ensuring the permanence of savings funds as a renewable financial resource requires a robust investment governance and risk-management framework. Indeed, natural resource funds that are poorly governed risk destroying capital and providing opportunities for corruption.

- *Policy makers need to manage the trade-off between investing in the domestic economy or abroad, and saving for future generations. In order to do so they should consider: 1) the capital stock and level of development of a country, and 2) whether resource revenues are long lasting or temporary in light of the resource depletion rate.* Beyond the appropriate level of precautionary savings necessary to provide a financial buffer to ensure fiscal sustainability over time, the fiscal rules can be designed to favour current and medium-term expenditure of natural resource revenues or accumulating wealth for future generations in a savings fund, in a manner that is consistent with national development priorities, absorptive capacity constraints, and the volatility of natural resource revenues over the commodity price cycle. Countries where there is ample capital and where resource revenues are temporary may opt for accumulating sufficient financial savings for future generations. For countries where capital is scarce and where resource revenues are temporary, a balance should be struck between accumulating financial savings and spending resource revenue domestically to increase non-resource sector growth, also taking into account the borrowing position of the country on international markets. However, the decision to save for future generations must be set against the country's borrowing costs and debt dynamics. If the risk-adjusted return on long-term savings is less than the country's borrowing costs, the long-term savings represent a net loss for the country. For countries where there is ample capital and where resource revenues are long lasting, the priority should be on managing volatility and achieving macro-fiscal stability. For countries where capital is scarce and where resource revenues are long lasting, the priority should be to invest revenues domestically, while accounting for absorptive capacity constraints and maintaining macroeconomic stability. However, even if good investment opportunities exist in developing economies, issues around capabilities to choose and execute selected projects may arise. In such contexts, saving for future generations can be a prudent option while the necessary capabilities are built up.

Policy Challenge 2: How to transform finite natural resource revenues into long-standing and productive development gains, in order to put resource-rich developing countries on a sustainable development trajectory that outlives resource extraction.

Recommended policy responses:

When prioritising spending on domestic investment over saving:

- Policy makers need to ensure commitment on the part of the government, a strategic vision, and a clear long-term development plan that informs spending and investment decisions and recognises the inherent volatility and finitude of natural resource revenues and absorptive capacity constraints. Any prioritisation of development-related expenditure which underwrites broad-based and inclusive development must be preceded by a commitment to sound and consistent macroeconomic management of natural resource revenues (see recommended policy responses to address Policy Challenge 1).

- Policy makers need to avoid spending mechanisms that encourage procyclicality in public expenditures as this exacerbates the effects of commodity price volatility on the economy. Earmarking can encourage procyclicality and constrain budgetary flexibility, lead to inefficiency and over or underinvestment in certain public services. Without concomitant stabilisation mechanisms, direct distribution through cash transfers are also highly procyclical and may divert revenues from priority investments at scale such as in infrastructure, health and education. At the same time, targeted cash-transfer schemes that operate through the government budget may be useful to smooth the transition for gradually phasing out fossil fuel subsidies, which tend to be poorly targeted and inefficient, yet popularly supported and thus often difficult to reform.

- Policy makers need to ensure the quality and efficiency of public investment spending, including through the choice of appropriate spending mechanisms to translate natural resource wealth into productive capital accumulation, leading to broader development gains. Strategic investment funds can help natural resource-rich countries manage long-term financing challenges and shrinking fiscal space, while balancing policy and commercial objectives. With their double bottom-line objective, whereby all investment decisions must fulfil market-based risk and return criteria, and produce positive development outcomes, strategic investment funds offer a possible tool for resource-rich countries to catalyse economic development, alongside conventional spending via the budget. Such funds are most effective as part of a clear government investment policy that establishes the priorities, criteria and targets for investment, coupled with some level of co-ordination across government levels and different agencies to avoid duplication of public investment.

Notes

[1] For example, the typical portfolio of a stabilisation fund is not significantly different from a foreign exchange reserve portfolio managed by a central bank. For this reason, stabilisation funds are often managed within existing government agencies, often with the central bank acting as the asset manager for the Ministry of Finance. Conventional government agencies are not, however, normally designed and resourced to invest directly or delegate investment management contracts in a larger range of asset classes of different risk profiles in public and private markets. For natural resource funds with longer investment time horizons and a greater short to medium-term risk tolerance, a special-purpose investment agency may be better placed to access and to maximise risk-adjusted returns over the long term.

[2] The FMP is a public trust of the Ministry of Finance and the Central Bank is appointed to act as a trustee. Under this scheme, the corporate governance of the FMP rests with the technical committee that performs various duties related to the receipt of hydrocarbon revenues, investment management, and spending. The committee appoints an executive co-ordinator of

the FMP who manages the financial aspects of the contracts, including the calculation and execution of the payments derived from them to different parties. The committee determines the investment and risk-management policies for the long-run reserve. The committee instructs the staff to execute the transfers to the federal government. The committee approves its annual budget and working programme. If and when the long-run reserve exceeds 3% of GDP, the committee proposes to the congress an allocation of additional transfers amongst several pre-specified purposes (e.g. amount to the universal pension system vs. investments in science). The committee must also comment on the federal government's proposal for the size of the state dividend from Pemex (the national oil company).

[3] See International Monetary Fund "Ghana: 2017 Article IV Consultation".

[4] See Jones, T. (2016) 'The fall and rise of Ghana's debt: how a new debt trap has been set', https://jubileedebt.org.uk/wp-content/uploads/2016/10/The-fall-and-rise-of-Ghanas-debt_10.16.pdf (last accessed 14 January 2019).

[5] See Republic of Ghana (2016), *Annual Report on the Petroleum Funds*, available at: https://www.mofep.gov.gh/sites/default/files/reports/petroleum/2016%20Annual%20report%20on%20the%20Petroleum%20Funds.pdf (last accessed 14 January 2019).

[6] The Nigeria Sovereign Investment Authority (NSIA) established in 2011 also has a stabilisation portfolio. However, the NSIA does not receive hydrocarbon revenues directly, and has only received small disbursements from the budget twice totalling significantly less than 1% of GDP. With such limited financial resources in relation to GDP, the stabilisation function of the NSIA is very limited.

[7] For a fuller account of Kazakhstan's economic development, please see OECD report "Reforming Kazakhstan: Progress, Challenges and Opportunities", available at https://www.oecd.org/eurasia/countries/OECD-Eurasia-Reforming-Kazakhstan-EN.pdf.

[8] Despite strong economic growth, Botswana is still one of the world's most unequal countries, with high levels of extreme poverty, behind only South Africa and Seychelles. See World Bank (2015), *Botswana Poverty Assessment*, World Bank Group, Washington, DC.

[9] In 1993, Botswana established the Pula Fund with the objective of preserving part of the income from diamond exports for future generations, managing foreign exchange reserves that are more than the expected needs over the medium term, and mitigating Dutch-disease effects by holding the portfolio in foreign-denominated assets. This buffer came in useful for the government following the 2008/09 global financial crisis, which affected the diamond trade. The government drew on the fund to support expenditure to smooth the economic shock of the crisis on the economy. Managed as a distinct account at the central bank, the fund invests in public equity and fixed-income instruments in industrialised economies, with an aim of maximising investment returns subject to acceptable levels of risk. The fund does not invest in commodity-exporting countries to hedge against decreases in commodity prices. The Pula Fund has USD 5.4 billion in assets under management, or a third of GDP. As such, accumulated assets are small considering how long the country has been saving mineral revenues. What it shows, moreover, is that the country has focused on investing mineral revenues to improve the physical and human capital of the country.

[10] M-PESA served almost 12 million customers as of 2011 (over 50% of Kenya's adult population) and transferred approximately USD 415 million per month to individuals.

[11] Consider, for example, an individual that uses his/her cash transfer to purchase an automobile or some form of road transportation. The utility of this spending decision is contingent on a) the existence of a road network, and b) the quality of the road network.

[12] See Timor-Leste Ministry of Finance, "Petroleum Fund Legal Framework". Amended on 23 August 2011, http://www.mof.gov.tl/category/documents-and-forms/petroleum-fund-documents/petroleum-fund-legal-framework/?lang=en.

[13] See "Mineral Rights to Human Rights: Mobilising Resources from the Extractive Industries for Water, Sanitation and Hygiene. Case Study: Timor-Leste" (Oxford Policy Management, April 2017), 4. Available at: https://washmatters.wateraid.org/sites/g/files/jkxoof256/files/Mineral_rights_to_human_rights_mobilising_resources_from_the_Extractive_Industries_for_water_sanitation_and_hygiene.pdf (last accessed 7 October 2018).

[14] See, Neeraj Mittal, Anit Mukherjee and Alan Gelb, "Fuel Subsidy Reform in Developing Countries: Direct Benefit Transfer of LPG Cooking Gas Subsidy in India", *CGD Policy Paper*, Center for Global Development, Washington, DC, https://www.cgdev.org/publication/fuel-subsidy-reform-developing-countries-india.

[15] Some strategic investment funds invest in the extractives sector to increase its efficiency and productivity. For example, Abu Dhabi's Mubadala Development Corporation merged in 2016 with the Emirate's International Petroleum Investment Corporation, which is focused on upgrading productive capabilities in hydrocarbon development and processing.

[16] If, for example, the aim is to facilitate industrial and financial market development, these policy areas require complementary development. For instance, new sectors can be encouraged that create new job opportunities, but this relies in turn on the country's education and training regime to support the skills development of the workforce needed for the new sectors. If the aim is to attract foreign co-investors, this means creating a corporate governance and financial regulatory and oversight environment that they can trust. This does not mean that strategic investment funds are necessarily unsuccessful where the policy and regulatory environment is underdeveloped. Rather, a strategic investment fund works best in tandem with institutional development.

[17] Examples of sovereign wealth funds following this model, which is not typical, include the Kuwait Investment Authority, the State Oil Fund of the Republic of Azerbaijan, and the National Development Fund of Iran. There are several potential risks that can come from this residual model (see Bauer, 2015). First, using the sovereign wealth fund for domestic purposes may undermine its macroeconomic objectives, particularly around absorptive capacity. Second, it may undermine public financial management by bypassing the project appraisal, public procurement, and project monitoring standards used in the normal budget expenditure process. This may lead, moreover, to duplication and fragmentation of public investment, thus undermining the adequacy of public investment and spending on areas of greater social and infrastructural needs. Third, using the sovereign wealth fund for domestic investment may undermine public accountability. Spending and investment via the government budget allows for parliamentary scrutiny and accountability. Excluding domestic investment limits the possibility that sovereign wealth fund capital will be funnelled to projects and entities that serve the interests of those making the decisions.

[18] This classification is taken from Allen and Radev (2010:1), which defines extra-budgetary entities (or units) as, "institutions that are engaged in extra-budgetary transactions, may use extra-budgetary accounts, may have their own governance structures and, often, a legal status that is independent of government ministries and departments."

[19] Governance and reporting structures vary. Some report directly to the Minister of Finance. In other cases, the fund is overseen by a governing council that includes government ministers. For example, the Ireland Strategic Investment Fund is controlled and managed by the National Treasury Management Agency, which reports to the Minister of Finance. In the case of the Nigeria Sovereign Investment Authority, its Board of Directors reports once a year to the

20. governing council, which includes the president of Nigeria, state governors, and other government ministers including finance. In the case of Abu Dhabi's Mubadala, the board is chaired by the crown prince, but the investment committee below it is responsible for developing and monitoring investment strategy and performance, which is then reported to the Board.

20. An example is Kazakhstan's Samruk-Kazyna, a joint-stock company established in 2008 that owns in part or in whole many important companies in Kazakhstan, such as KazMunyGas, the state-owned oil and gas company. The key difference between Samruk-Kazyna and the National Fund of the Republic of Kazakhstan (NFRK) is that the NFRK is invested mostly in low-risk foreign assets, whereas Samruk-Kazyna is invested in domestic assets with an aim of maximising the long-term value and competitiveness of its portfolio companies in international markets.

21. FONSIS defines strategic sectors following the *Plan Senegal Emergent*, which includes agriculture, fishing, infrastructure, logistics and industrial hubs, energy, social housing, mining, and services (IT, education, health, business parks, and tourism). See www.fonsis.org.

References

Acemoglu, D., S. Johnson and J.A. Robinson (2002), "Reversal of fortune: geography and institutions in the making of the modern world income distribution", *Quarterly Journal of Economics* 117 (4):1231-1294.

Acosta Mejía, A., V. Albornoz and M. Caridad Araujo (2009), "Institutional reform, budget politics, and fiscal outcomes in Ecuador", in *Who decides the budget? A political economy analysis of the budget process in Latin America*, eds. M. Hallerberg, C. Scartascini and E. Stein, pp. 123-156, Inter-American Development Bank, Washington, DC.

Alisjahbana, A. (2005), "Does Indonesia Have the Balance Right in Natural Resource Revenue-Sharing?", in *The Politics and Economics of Indonesia's Natural Resources*, ed. B. Resosudarmo, Institute of Southeast Asian Studies, Singapore.

Allen, R. and D. Radev (2010), *Extrabudgetary Funds*, International Monetary Fund, Washington.

Allen, R. and D. Tommasi eds. (2001), *Managing Public Expenditure A Reference Book for Transition Countries: A Reference Book for Transition Countries*, OECD Publishing, Paris.

Almeida, M., V. Gallardo and A. Tomaselli (2006), *Gobernabilidad fiscal en Ecuador*, CEPAL/ILPES. Santiago, Chile (57).

Ambachtsheer, K., R. Capelle and T. Scheibelhut (1998), "Improving Pension Fund Performance", *Financial Analysts Journal*, Vol. 54, No. 6, pp. 15-21.

Ammann, M. and A. Zingg (2010), "Performance and Governance of Swiss Pension Funds", *Journal of Pension Economics and Finance*, Vol. 9, No. 1, pp. 95-128.

Ang, A (2010), "The Four Benchmarks of Sovereign Wealth Funds",(21 September 2010). Available at SSRN: https://ssrn.com/abstract=1680485 or http://dx.doi.org/10.2139/ssrn.1680485.

Arnold, C., T. Conway and M. Greenslade (2011), *Cash Transfers: Literature Review*, Department for International Development.

Arrellano-Yanguas, J. and A. Mejía Acosta (2014), "Extractives industries, revenue allocation and local politics", *UNRISD Working Paper* 2014 (4).

Bauer, A. (2015), "Six reasons why sovereign wealth funds should not invest or spend at home", in *Natural Resource Governance Institute Blog*, Natural Resource Governance Institute, New York.

Baunsgaard, T., M. Villafuente, M. Poplawski-Ribeiro and C. Richmond (2012), "Fiscal frameworks for resource rich developing countries", *IMF Staff Discussion Note* 12 (4).

Campi, A. (2012), "Mongolia's Quest to Balance Human Development in Its Booming Mineral-Based Economy", in *Brookings East Asia Commentary*, Brookings, Washington, DC.

Chambers, D., E. Dimson and A. Ilmanen (2012), "The Norway Model", *The Journal of Portfolio Management*, Vol. 38, No. 2, pp. 67-81.

Clark, G.L (2007), "Expertise and Representation in Financial Institutions: UK Legislation on Pension Fund Governance and US Regulation of the Mutual Fund Industry", *Twenty-first Century Society*, Vol. 2, No. 1, pp. 1-23.

Clark, G.L. and R.C. Urwin (2008), "Best-Practice Pension Fund Governance", *Journal of Asset Management*, Vol. 9, No. 1, pp. 2-21.

Collier, P., F. van der Ploeg, M. Spence and A. Venables (2010), "Managing Resource Revenues in Developing Economies", *IMF Staff Papers*, Vol. 57, pp. 84-118.

Corden, W (1984), "Booming Sector and Dutch Disease Economics: Survey and Consolidation", *Oxford Economic Papers*, Vol. 36, No. 3, pp. 359-380.

Cueva, S. and M. Ortiz (2013), *Ingresos fiscales por explotación de hidrocaburos en Ecuador*, Inter-American Development Bank (198).

Dimson, E., P. Marsh and M. Staunton (2002), *Triumph of the Optimists: 101 Years of Global Investment Returns*, Princeton University Press, Princeton, N.J., Oxford.

Das, U.S., A. Mazarei and H. van der Hoorn (eds.) (2010), *Economics of Sovereign Wealth Funds: Issues for Policymakers*, International Monetary Fund, Washington, DC.

Duflo, E. (2001), "Schooling and Labor Market Consequences of School Construction in Indonesia: Evidence from an Unusual Policy Experiment", *The American Economic Review* 91 (4):795-813.

Fama, E. and K. French (2002), "The Equity Premium", *The Journal of Finance*, Vol. 57, No. 2, pp. 637-659.

Fasano-Filho, U (2000), "Review of the Experience with Oil Stabilization and Savings Funds in Selected Countries", *IMF Working Papers*.

Frankel, J.A. (2010), "The natural resource curse: a survey", *National Bureau of Economic Research Working Paper Series* No. 15836.

Gelb, A. (2012), "Economic diversification in resource rich countries", In *Beyond the curse: policies to harness the power of natural resources*, ed. A. Sy, R. Arezki, T. Gylfason, International Monetary Fund, Washington, DC.

Gelb, A., S. Tordo, H. Halland, N. Arfaa and G. Smith (2014), "Sovereign wealth funds and long-term development finance: risks and opportunities", *World Bank Policy Research Working Paper* (6776).

Gelb, A.H. (1988), *Oil windfalls: blessing or curse?*, Published for the World Bank [by] Oxford University Press, New York, Oxford.

Gelpern, A. (2011), "Sovereignty, Accountability, and the Wealth Fund Governance Conundrum", *Asian Journal of International Law* 1 (2):289-320.

Goetzmann, W.N. and R.G. Ibbotson (2006), *The Equity Risk Premium: Essays and Explorations*, Oxford University Press, Oxford; New York.

Gupta, S., A. Segura-Ubiergo and E. Flores (2014), "Direct Distribution of Resource Revenues: Worth Considering?", *IMF Discussion Note* SDN/14/05.

Gylfason, T (2001), "A Nordic Perspective on Natural Resource Abundance", in R.M. Auty (ed.), *Resource Abundance and Economic Development*, 296-311, Oxford University Press, Oxford.

Iglesias, A. and R.J. Palacios (2000), *Managing Public Pension Reserves-Part I: Evidence from the International Experience*, World Bank, Washington, DC.

Isakova, A., A. Plekhanov and J. Zettelmeyer (2012), "Managing Mongolia's resource boom", *European Bank for Reconstruction and Development Working Papers* (138).

Kemme, D. (2012), "Sovereign wealth fund issues and the national fund(s) of Kazakhstan", *William Davidson Institute Working Papers* (1036).

Khalaf, R., L. Saigol and H. Sender (2011), "The two faces of Libya's investment fund", *Financial Times*, London.

Knapp, G., S. Goldsmith, A. Kruse and G. Erickson (1984), *The Alaska Permanent Fund Dividend Program: Economic Effects and Public Attitudes*, Institute of Social and Economic Research, University of Alaska.

Lopez Murphy, P., M. Villafuerte and R. Ossowski (2010), *Riding the Roller Coaster; Fiscal Policies of Nonrenewable Resource Exporters in Latin America and the Caribbean*, International Monetary Fund.

Mitchell, O.S. and P.L. Hsin (1997), "Public Pension Governance and Performance", in S. Valdes-Prieto (ed.), *The Economics of Pensions: Principles, Policies, and International Experience*, 92-126, Cambridge University Press, Cambridge.

Moss, T., C. Lambert and S. Majerowicz (2015), *Oil to Cash: Fighting the Resource Curse through Cash Transfers*, Brookings Institution Press, Washington, DC.

Norton, J.J. (2010), "The Santiago Principles for Sovereign Wealth Funds: A Case Study on International Financial Standard-Setting Processes", *Journal of International Economic Law* 13 (3):645-662.

Romano, R (1993), "Public Pension Fund Activism in Corporate Governance Reconsidered", *Columbia Law Review*, Vol. 93, No. 4, pp. 795-853.

Saigol, L. and C. O'Murchu (2011), "After Gaddafi: A spent force", *Financial Times*, Pearson, London.

Solow, R.M (1986), "On the Intergenerational Allocation of Natural Resources", *The Scandinavian Journal of Economics*, Vol. 88, No. 1, pp. 141-149.

Tornell, A. and P.R. Lane (1999), "The Voracity Effect", *The American Economic Review*, Vol. 89, No. 1, pp. 22-46.

Truman, E.M. (2010), *Sovereign wealth funds: threat or salvation?*, Peterson Institute for International Economics, Washington, DC.

Yanez-Pagans, M. (2008), "Culture and Human Capital Investments: Evidence of an Unconditional Cash Transfer Program in Bolivia", in *IZA Discussion Papers*, Institute for the Study of Labor (IZA).

Yeung, Y. and S. Howes (2015), "Resources-to-Cash: a Cautionary Tale from Mongolia", in *Development Policy Centre Discussion Papers*, Australian National University.

www.ingramcontent.com/pod-product-compliance
Lightning Source LLC
LaVergne TN
LVHW062000070526
838199LV00060B/4205